FACT FILES

MAPS

What You Need to Know

by LINDA CROTTA BRENNAN

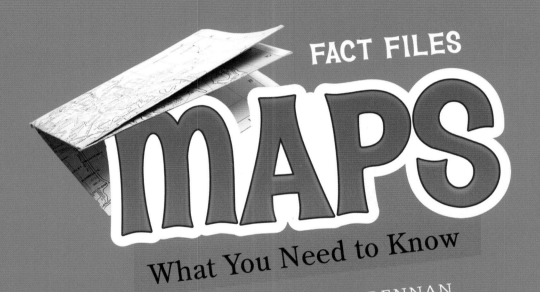

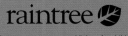
raintree

a Capstone company — publishers for children

Raintree is an imprint of Capstone Global Library Limited, a company incorporated in England and Wales having its registered office at 264 Banbury Road, Oxford, OX2 7DY – Registered company number: 6695582

www.raintree.co.uk
myorders@raintree.co.uk

Edited by Mandy Robbins
Designed by Jenny Bergstrom
Picture research by Kelly Garvin
Production by Laura Manthe
Originated by Capstone Global Library Limited
Printed and bound in China.

ISBN 978-1-4747-4889-6
21 20 19 18 17
10 9 8 7 6 5 4 3 2 1

British Library Cataloguing in Publication Data
A full catalogue record for this book is available from the British Library.

Acknowledgements

Shutterstock: Artlisticco, 13, Betacam-SP, 9 (bottom right), Cvijun, 7, dikobraziy, 21, Dja65, 4, dvoevnore, 8, Eka Panova, 6, ergonomal, cover (top right), 19, freesoulproduction, cover (top left), Globe Turner, 9 (bottom left), HomeStudio, cover (br), 1, lcatnews, 5, mstudioVector, 15, Oleksandr Berezko, 17, oxameel, 9 (tl), pablofdezr, 9 (tr), pavalena, 11, Peter Hermes Furian, 15, prokopphoto, 24, Scanrail1, 3, Triff, cover (bl), Zmiter, backcover, 12

Contents

Introduction to maps.................... 4

Types of maps 6

Parts of a map.......................... 10

Maps of the world...................... 16

Try to find it 20

Glossary 22

Read more 23

Websites.................................23

Critical thinking questions 24

Index.....................................24

Introduction to maps

Where are you right now? Where do you want to go next? A map can help you get there.

A map is a drawing of what an area looks like from above. Maps use lines, colours and pictures to tell you about a place.

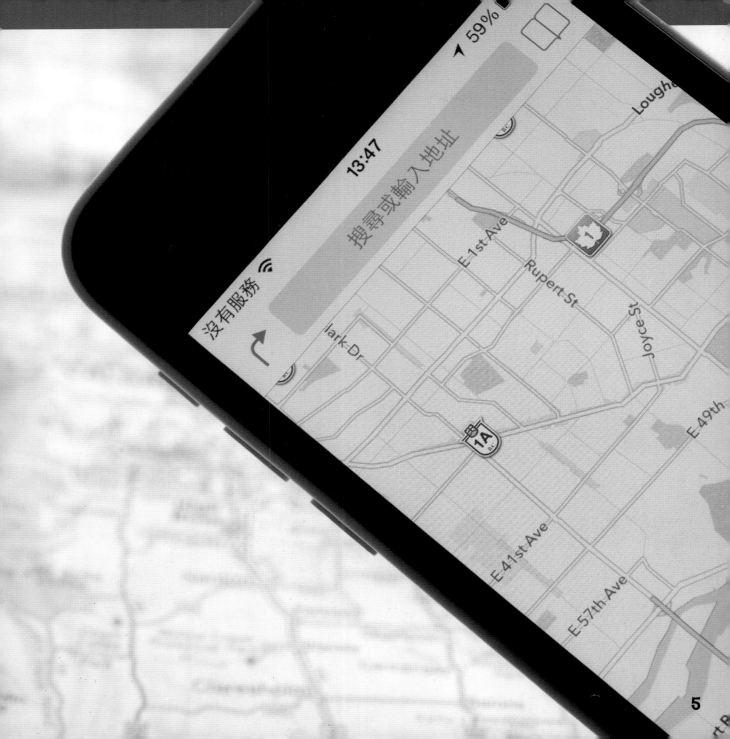

Types of maps

You couldn't use a map of Earth to find your way around school. To get where you need to go, you must have the right map.

Some maps show the whole world or an entire country. But what if you want to find the local hospital? For that you need a map of your city or town.

HOSPITAL

WORLD MAP

N
W E
S

THIS MAP SHOWS ALL THE COUNTRIES OF THE WORLD.

CAN YOU FIND THE COUNTRY
YOU LIVE IN?

7

There are many types of maps. Political maps show countries. Road maps show roads and cities. Historical maps show what places looked like long ago. There are also maps of the sea and the stars.

FACT
The maps that pilots and sailors use are called charts.

SEA CHART

STAR CHART

POLITICAL MAP

ROAD MAP

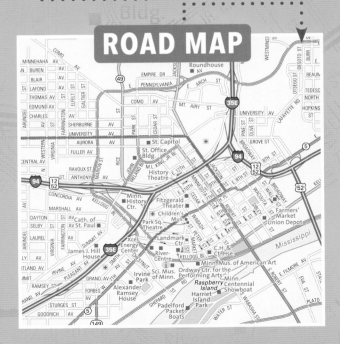

HISTORICAL MAP

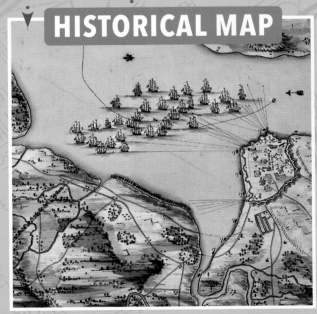

Parts of a map

Maps use colours and symbols to give information. A map's **key** tells you what its colours and symbols mean. On most maps, blue means water.

Some maps show **elevation**. Brown means highlands. Yellow and orange stand for middle lands. Green means low lands.

key – a list or chart that explains the colours and symbols on a map
elevation – the height of the land above sea level

Baltic Sea

North Sea

Sylt

Hamburg

Bremen

Hanover

★ Berlin

Elbe

Leipzig

Cologne

Dresden

GERMANY

Rhine

Koblenz

Frankfurt

Mainz

Heidelberg

Danube

Stuttgart

Freudenstadt

Munich

Freiberg

MAP OF GERMANY

WHICH CITY IS THE

CAPITAL

OF GERMANY?

NAME A

RIVER

IN GERMANY.

KEY

∫ **RIVER**

● **CITY**

★ **CAPITAL CITY**

Capital city: Berlin
Rivers: Rhine, Danube, Elbe

Most maps have *compass roses*.
A compass rose is a circle with arrows that split it into four equal parts. The arrows point in the directions north, east, south and west.

compass rose – a label that shows the directions north, east, south and west on a map
compass – an instrument used for finding directions

KEY

Entrance	Horses	Tigers
Fountain	Camels	Cheetahs
Toilets	Birds	Flamingos
Food	Turtles	Snakes
Monkeys	Hippos	
Rhinos	Lions	

SEARCH

You are at the zoo by the lions. You want to see the monkeys. Should you go north, east, south or west?

13

Maps are smaller than the places they show. The map's **scale** tells you how much smaller the map is than real life.

Some maps have **grids** to help you find a place. Grids are evenly spaced lines that run up-and-down and side-to-side.

scale – a label on the map that compares the distances on a map and the actual distances on Earth
grid – a pattern of evenly spaced, or parallel, lines that cross

On this map 2.5 centimetres is equal to 500 kilometres.

MEASURE

the centimetres between Alice Springs and Mackay.

HOW MANY

kilometres are there between the two towns? Mackay is in section 5C. In what

SECTION

of the grid is Alice Springs?

15

Maps of the world

Most maps are flat. It makes them easy to fold up and carry. But the world is shaped like a ball. To make a world map flat, countries are shown stretched and pulled out of shape. A *globe* is a map that shows Earth's round shape. It gives a more true picture of Earth.

FACT

There are seven **continents** on Earth: Africa, Antarctica, Asia, Australia, Europe, North America and South America.

globe – a round model of the world
continent – one of the seven large land masses of Earth

A globe has special lines. Those that run up-and-down are lines of **longitude**. Those that run sideways are lines of **latitude**. The line around the centre of the globe is called the **equator**. The point at the top of the globe is the North Pole. The point at the bottom is the South Pole.

longitude – the position of a place, measured in degrees east or west of an imaginary line that runs through Greenwich, England

latitude – the position of a place, measured in degrees north or south of the equator

equator – an imaginary line around the middle of Earth; it divides the northern and southern hemispheres

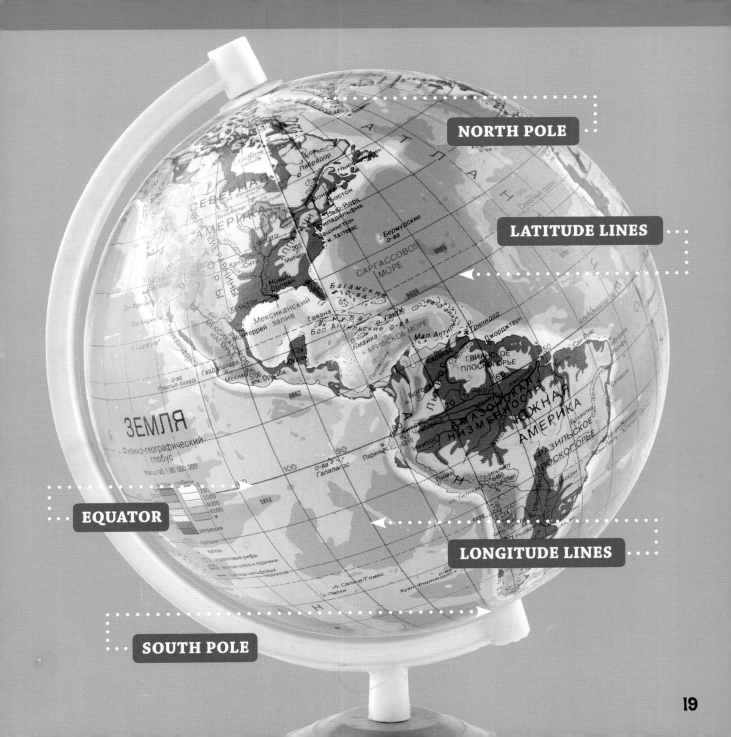

NORTH POLE

LATITUDE LINES

EQUATOR

LONGITUDE LINES

SOUTH POLE

Try to find it

Maps can help you find your way on land, at sea or even in space. So grab a map and explore!

Earth has four oceans. They are the Arctic, Atlantic, Indian and Pacific oceans. Can you find the Atlantic Ocean on this world map?

Australia is east of the Indian Ocean. Can you find both on this map?

On what continent is Mount Everest?

WORLD MAP

ARCTIC OCEAN

N
W   E
S

Rocky Mountains

NORTH AMERICA

Mississippi River

ATLANTIC OCEAN

PACIFIC OCEAN

Amazon River

SOUTH AMERICA

Andes Mountains

EUROPE

Ural Mountains

ASIA

AFRICA

Mount Everest

INDIAN OCEAN

AUSTRALIA

KEY

- ⬭ WATER
- ⋀⋀ MOUNTAINS
- ∫ RIVER
- ▲ MOUNT

ANTARCTICA

Glossary

compass an instrument used for finding directions

compass rose a label that shows direction on a map

continent one of the seven large land masses of Earth

elevation the height of the land above sea level

equator an imaginary line around the middle of Earth

globe a round model of the world

grid a pattern of evenly spaced, or parallel, lines that cross

key a list or chart that explains colours or symbols on a map

latitude the distance measured north or south of the equator

longitude the distance measured east or west of a line that runs through Greenwich, England; lines of longitude are drawn from the North Pole to the South Pole

scale a label on the map that compares the distances on a map and the actual distances on Earth

Read more

Children's Discovery Atlas, Anita Ganeri (QED Publishing, 2017)

Children's Illustrated World Atlas (Children's Illustrated Atlas) (DK, 2017)

My Country (Mapping), Jen Green (Wayland, 2017)

You Are Here; Maps and Why We Use Them (Collins Big Cat), Isabel Thomas (Collins, 2017)

Websites

www.bbc.co.uk/education/clips/zc6yr82

Visit this BBC website to watch a video clip that shows how to use a compass and how to read maps.

www.nationalgeographic.com/kids-world-atlas/maps.html

This National Geographic website has free maps to download.

www.ordnancesurvey.co.uk/mapzone/

Visit the Ordnance Survey's interactive website to learn map skills.

Critical thinking questions

1. What kind of map shows states and countries?

2. What parts of a map can be found on the map on page 11?

3. On a world map, find the country where you live. Would it take longer for you to travel to Spain or to Mexico? How do you know?

Index

compass roses 12

elevation maps 10

equator 18

globes 16, 18

grids 14

historical maps 8

keys 10

latitude 18

longitude 18

political maps 8

road maps 8

scale 14

sea charts 8

star charts 8

world maps 6, 16, 18, 20